Sweet Kare

WEALTH CODES COACH
INTRODUCES

LIMITLESS LIVING
TODAY

with

DAILY ENCOURAGEMENTS

S + L

ROB SAUNDERS

Oct 10, 2017

Cover Design: Carlos Bido
Creative Editor: Maria Erokhina
Publishing Editor: Polly Harder

DEDICATION

This book is dedicated to those who desire to meditate upon the wisdom of the CEO of the Universe. This wisdom is revealed in His Word, which contains many powerful Wealth Codes, Covenants and Blessings. You will find many of them on these pages.

God originally intended for us to enjoy every day without the fear of failure and lack. It's time to start living in the infinity of God's best intentions toward us, which ultimately lead straight into eternal life.

Surely the word LIMITLESS describes God.

Shouldn't it also characterize our vision and expectations?

We all experience conflicts surrounding our pursuit of Limitless Living. In fact, we must expect challenges, troubles and trials; and in this world they are increasing. Yeshua told us we can't avoid them. However, He also encouraged us to rejoice and be of good cheer in the midst of tribulations and rapid chaotic change. This book provides us with Wealth Codes and daily encouragements, which will lead us to break out into a limitless life.

Today let's enter into God's favor and blessings, for with them He adds no sorrow, toil or pain. His Covenants and Commands will raise us to soar above the strife-filled, unhappy and quickly changing world.

" I will give you
the treasures of darkness,
the hidden wealth of secret places,
so you may know
It is I, The Lord . . . "
(Isaiah 45:3)

TABLE OF CONTENTS

WHAT IS A WEALTH CODE?

INTRODUCTION

WEALTH CODES AUDIT

3 MINUTE DAILY ENCOURAGEMENTS

WHAT ARE WEALTH CODES?

- Wealth Codes aren't first about money, but about "hidden" thoughts and ways of God that will enrich your life.

- Wealth Codes reveal the Wisdom that creates a more meaningful, rewarding and precious life.

- Wealth Codes explain God's Covenants and Blessings, giving assurance—getting results.

- Wealth Codes convey warnings that will spare you, and advice that will save you.

- Wealth Codes bring Happiness, 'Love & Laughter'— so enjoy them.

- Wealth Codes uncover God's continual and eternal generosity toward you.

- Wealth Codes enlarge your vision so that you can walk in ways that are new to you.

- Wealth Codes define the quality and purpose of life found in the Kingdom of Heaven.

- Wealth Codes prove the laws of the Kingdom of Heaven operate in the midst of storms and tribulations.

Happy, Confident, Fortunate,
Blessed, Healthy and Wise
is everyone who gains
the Power of the Wealth Codes.

INTRODUCTION

Of first importance, Wealth Codes are found throughout God's Word. These Revelations, Covenants and Blessings, though costly to obtain, constantly revolutionize my life. I enjoy waking up in God's world, full of dreams, hope and creative energy. I am confident, knowing His brighter future waits for me.

Now, of course, we will always have trials to face, temptations to overcome and valleys to cross on this chaotic and stress-filled Earth. But when you discover and break open the Wealth Codes, contained herein, your life will become more vibrant and optimistic. Hope will appear.

Limitless Life and its habits are better caught than taught. These essential, life-changing Wealth Codes come from proven experience. It's my joy to share these Daily Encouragements for the next 31 days. Let them 'soak in' one at a time. And then, review your favorites often.

Be encouraged—throw back your curtains and walk onto a new stage of life—free—with renewable energy.

Start now! Wonderful adventures await you.
Begin your LIMITLESS LIFE TODAY.

*Before you start your 3 minute daily journey, please take a Wealth Codes Audit on the next two pages. Reflect upon your answers. They will give you a clear starting point.

WEALTH CODES AUDIT

"You may say in your heart, 'My power and my hand made me this wealth.' But don't forget it is the Lord your God, Who gave you power to make your wealth, confirming His Covenant which He swore to your fathers, as it is this day" (Deuteronomy 8:17, 18).

- My total dependence on God makes me happy, successful and abundant.

  ALWAYS   SOMETIMES   NEVER

- I confirm that it is God's Covenant that gives me the power to make my wealth.

  ALWAYS   SOMETIMES   NEVER

- My 'first purpose' is to be about my Father's Business —House—Purpose.

  ALWAYS   SOMETIMES   NEVER

- I reject the temptation to serve two supreme masters —only God—not the lord Mamonas/Money.

  ALWAYS   SOMETIMES   NEVER

WEALTH CODES AUDIT

"Yeshua answered, 'Why is it you were looking for me? You must know that I first have to be about My Father's house—business—affairs'" (Luke 2:49).

• I refuse to let the deceitfulness of riches force me into the limits of the Business Hamster Wheel.

   ALWAYS   SOMETIMES   NEVER

• I only walk through the doors God opens for me—no one can shut those!

   ALWAYS   SOMETIMES   NEVER

• For me, no amount of money is worth the risk of becoming a 'financial hostage.'

   ALWAYS   SOMETIMES   NEVER

• I avoid getting so busy that I don't have time to wait upon the Lord for my answers.

   ALWAYS   SOMETIMES   NEVER

If you answered 'Sometimes or Never' to at least 4 of these 8, you immediately need to start reading this book.

THE HAPPY AND LIMITLESS HEART

"It is the blessing of the Lord that makes one rich, and
He adds no sorrow, toil or pain with it"
(Proverbs 10:22).

Open your eyes to
**Real & Limitless
Heart Riches**

The Kingdom of Heaven is like a merchant seeking
fine pearls and upon finding one of great value, he
sold all that he had and bought it (Matthew 13:45).

To discover the Pearl of Great Price
is to gain a happy heart and find limitless youth!

*For today's encouragement, I seek Your blessings and
priceless pearls I've never dreamed of.*

RICHES AND SO MUCH MORE

atthew McConnaughy said about the movie Gold, "In America, we call success fame and money." However, Katherine Kuhlman stated, "There is so much more!" She understood this 'American mentality' well—even her beloved father mostly wanted money.

I've been in over 100 business deals, including buying many companies. Trying to force all the moving parts to work together often made me worn out. That work seemed like "hard labor" and a "consuming fire."

Today I avoid those exhausting and limiting types of investments. I've learned the gigantic value of not doing business "my way." Of course, there will be problems from time to time in all business deals, but we can measure our success by the fulfillment these opportunities bring into our lives. Remember, the generosity of the Lord's blessings comes without toil, hurt and sorrow. These are all parts of God's Covenant.

Let's talk to the Lord and listen for His voice . . .

Lord, we need encouragement today. Teach us the real benefit of Your limitless true riches. Increase our faith and willingness to know and do Your will. Fulfill Your plans and purposes for our work life and business.

WHAT LIMITLESS WISH?

"The blind man called out, saying, 'Jesus, Son of
David, have mercy on me!' Jesus stopped and
commanded, 'Bring him to Me!' Then He asked,
'WHAT DO YOU WISH Me to do for you?'"
(Luke 18:35-43).

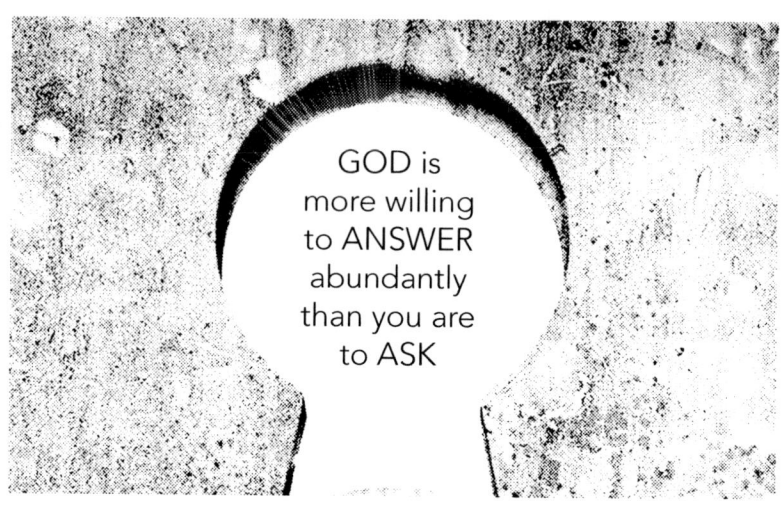

GOD is
more willing
to ANSWER
abundantly
than you are
to ASK

"Call out to Me, and I will answer you, and I will
tell (and teach) you great and mighty things,
which you do not know" (Jeremiah 33:3).

*I am encouraged—my mind is turned upside down
today—as I meditate on the truth that You are
limitless and more willing to answer my requests fully
than I am to ask them.*

ACCEPT NO LIMITS

Everyone stopped to hear the conversation between the blind man and Yeshua. The secret was that the God of Creation saw the blind man as to who and what he could be—and connected with his heart. What a gracious and generous gift The Son of God had in mind for the blind seeker. Yeshua gladly asked, "What do you want/wish Me to do for you?"

One day, I was studying this story when I realized this wonder: Heaven's will for us is so good. Yeshua was always asking what He could do for us—there were no limits! Heaven is on our side.

His Divine plan is: "Father God is willing to do—and can do—more exceedingly abundantly for us—beyond all that we ask or think—dream or imagine—according to His power working within us" (Ephesians 3:20).

Teach us to dream and imagine for more . . .

*Dear Lord, this day we want to hear You and
ACCEPT NO LIMITS.
Keep us from being faint-hearted. Reveal the great and
mighty things that will increase our faith. Give us a heart
of wisdom and zeal for a limitless life.*

HIS LIMITLESS COVENANT

DEUTERONOMY 8 IS REVOLUTIONARY:
"Remember the Lord your God
Who gives you
Power to Make Wealth . . ."

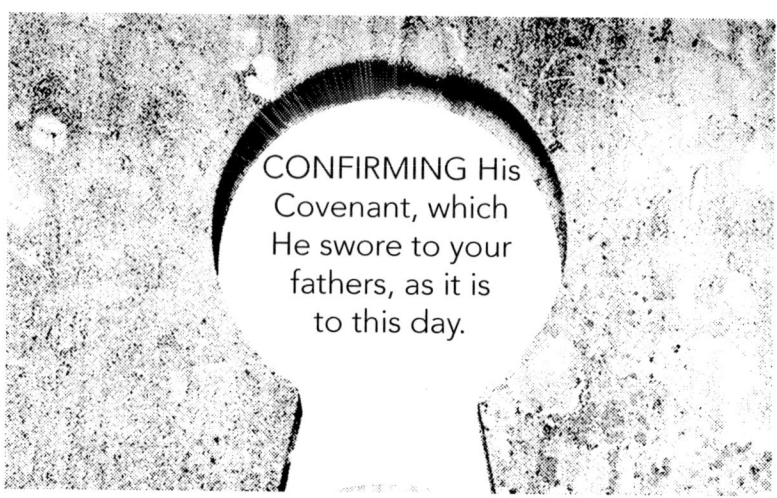

CONFIRMING His
Covenant, which
He swore to your
fathers, as it is
to this day.

"IF you say in your heart, 'My own power made me
this wealth' and forget the Lord your God . . .
I testify against you today
that you will surely perish."

*For today's meditation, I focus on the encouragement
of this Covenant. I am amazed that He alone gives me
the power to make True Wealth. I break free from the
limitations and danger that 'my way' brings.*

THE POWER TO MAKE WEALTH

What a marvelous Covenant we have inherited, but it seems to be rarely considered.

There is also a big "IF"—"IF you ever forget—and go after other gods and serve and worship them"—a terrible drama will be your end!

The GOD OF GOLD often causes this drama. Under that god's influence, how can Gold be neutral? (Exodus 32:31)

My trouble was making wealth by my own power and cleverness, which limited God's best options. I did achieve my goals, but I paid a terrible price for my independence.

I now look first to His limitless power and favor, bringing His blessings to me. The 'test question' remains: Will I use the money and success for His purpose first?

Let's talk to the Lord and listen for His voice . . .

Lord, we wonder why we are so prone to follow the god of gold and our own will, knowing they lead to a fading glory. Encourage us to work within Your Covenant— Your way.

FIRST PURPOSE

At 12 years old, Yeshua's first recorded words expressed His First Purpose. "He said to His mother, 'Why is it you were looking for Me? You must know I have to be about My Father's Business—Affairs—House'" (Luke 2:49).

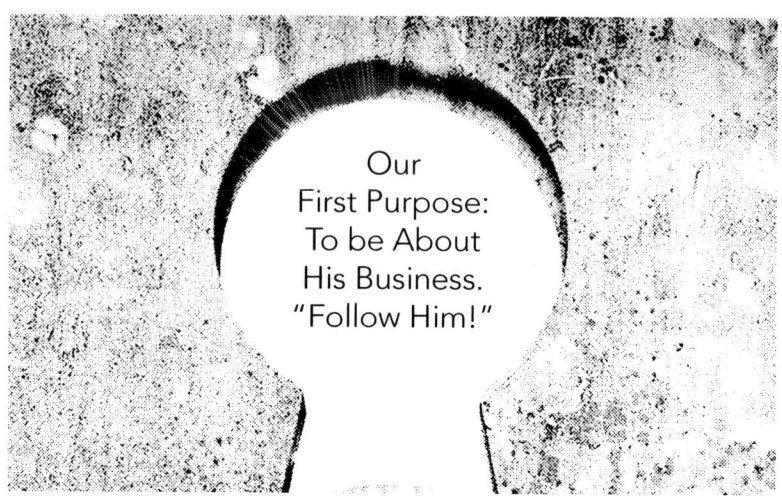

Our
First Purpose:
To be About
His Business.
"Follow Him!"

Refusing to be spiritually profitable ends in great loss. Instead, follow the best plans God has for you.

Today, I meditate on this wonderful Word, "The Lord, the God of your fathers, may increase you a thousand times more—limitlessly—and bless you as He has promised you" (Deuteronomy 1:11).

REWARDS FOLLOW PURPOSE

"... Your Reward shall be very great ...
Now look toward the *limitless* heavens,
and count the stars, if you can ..."
(Genesis 15:1-5).

Abraham's plans and actions unfolded out of
his First Purpose and Call.

He departed—God directed: GET OUT of Ur of the
Chaldeans! God needed him to move in order to bless
and show him all the rewards He had prepared for his
obedience.

It's the same for us all—following Yeshua is our greatest
reward. Once we earn His rewards by obedience, then
He will entrust us with more. It was not comfortable
or convenient for Abraham to leave his home. It's the
same with us. Seek first His Kingdom's business and
will, and you will be happy and fulfilled.

We are glad to come together today . . .

*We seek to know Your purpose. It seems obvious
to us that we do things backwards
—we seek first our will—
Lord, help us out of this contradiction.
Encountering You—we have nothing to fear.*

HAPPY AND PROSPEROUS

"Happy, blessed, prosperous and to be admired are those who are poor in spirit, for theirs is the Kingdom of Heaven" (Matthew 5:3).

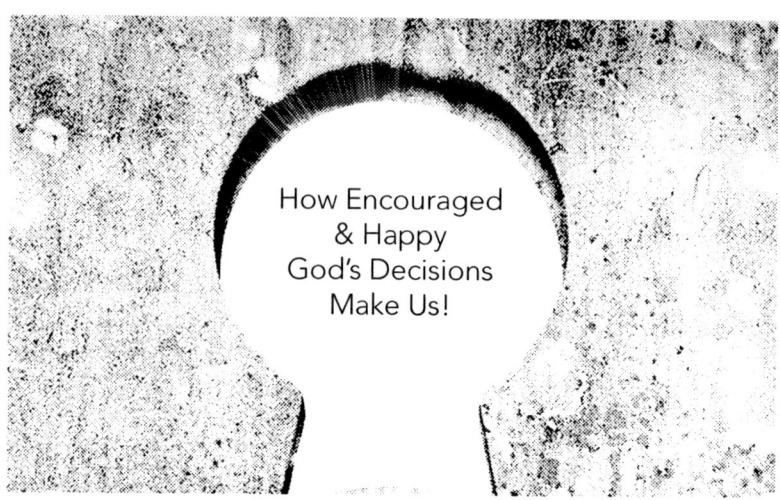

How Encouraged
& Happy
God's Decisions
Make Us!

I asked someone I trusted, "What does it mean to be 'poor in spirit?'" They answered, "Robert, the poor in spirit are those who seek God for their answers and do not trust in their own wisdom."

Now I stop, get still and consider that total dependence on God's Spirit makes me happy and prosperous. What a wonderful encouragement to start the day with!

THE POOR IN SPIRIT

Frankly, I was never very attracted to the term "poor in spirit." It ranked along with what John the Baptist said, "He must increase, and I must decrease."

But now, so many years later, I really believe that the only way to happiness and enjoying what we have is through seeking to be poor in spirit. For then we find God's will and safety in the Kingdom of Heaven. There we can obtain peace, prosperity and happiness.

God's Words are always true, even though very challenging at first. Our happy and secret place of escape is where we will find hidden riches and meet all of our difficulties in Love & Laughter. Remember, it is the last few yards that count. If we trust God's Spirit, He will not fail us. However, we are sure the world's commercial advantages will.

As we come to pray, we remember . . .

How risky it is to act for ourselves—thinking God's too late to help us. Keep us from making the mistake of handling every detail, making every decision—becoming 'rich in spirit'—putting ourselves at risk of 'gaining the world's glitter and losing our soul.'

COMMERCIAL ADVANTAGES

The Romans believed they were divinely ordained to rule the world and tax all commerce. The cost to profit from Roman commerce meant worshipping the Caesar and the numerous gods of the Pantheon.

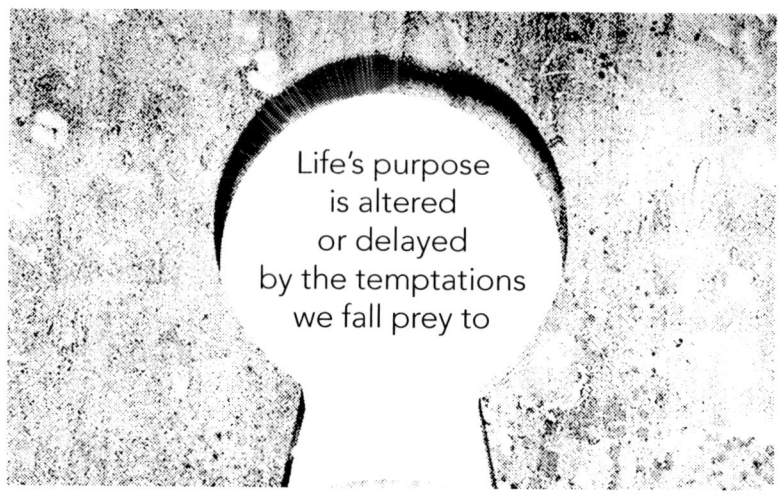

Life's purpose
is altered
or delayed
by the temptations
we fall prey to

Unfortunately, I often yielded to 'Rome's might and commercial advantages' if I knew I could gain wealth.

(Learn more about the conflict of Matthew, the tax collector. Breaking The Wealth Code, sections 1 and 2.)

Now in silence, I focus on my purpose. I do not want it delayed or changed by unexpected temptations today.

GIVE UNTO CAESAR

Ultimately it seems that important matters center around money and taxes. They asked Yeshua, "What do you think—is it lawful to pay a tax to Caesar?"

The 'Caesars' and 'empires' of the world force their way into the center of our lives. The 'test question' is: How do we do business 'before Caesar,' and yet not become tempted, entangled or obligated to serve him, thus losing our First allegiance to God?

Today, as we come and consider these matters in prayer, we desire to hear His still, small voice, which calls us back to remember: "Seek first My Kingdom and My righteousness and all these other 'Roman' things will be added unto you" (Matthew 6:33). Trusting in this truth sets us free from many business traps.

Father God, let us hear Your encouraging voice . . .

. . . so we escape the terror caused by any entanglement with the gods and 'Caesars' of this world and the desires for their things. Please Father, may Your will be accomplished in our lives. Keep us close—never let us go!

THE BUSINESS TRAP

"The worries of the world, the Deceitfulness of Riches, and the desires for other things enter in and choke . . . " (Mark 4:19).

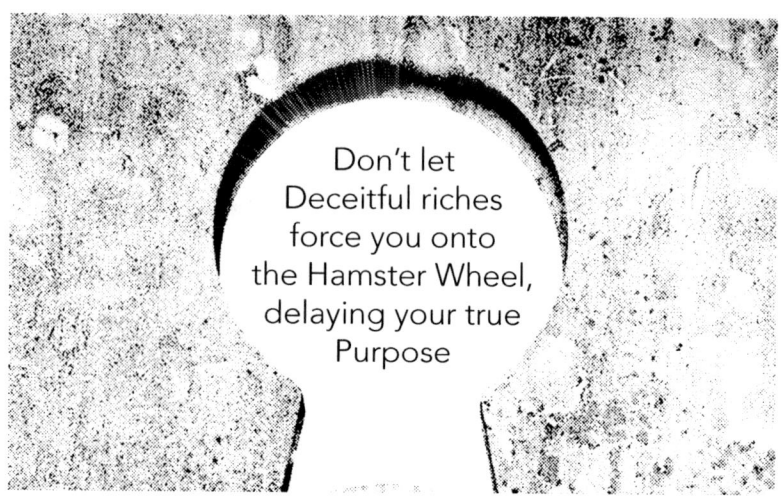

Don't let Deceitful riches force you onto the Hamster Wheel, delaying your true Purpose

Matthew became agitated, "Susanna, wake up to reality. I am thankful for the Empire. It's very profitable to serve Caesar. My tax collection business is growing." (Breaking The Wealth Code, p.23)

I pause to think: it is exhausting for me to continue running on the Business Hamster Wheel. I resolve to enjoy my life daily.

FINANCIAL HOSTAGES

recently received this text from a young businessman: "I appreciate your encouragement, but unfortunately, I don't have time to wait upon the Lord. Right now I have too many notes on my desktop, too many tasks on my screen, too much work to do. But I'm glad you reminded me that God reigns above all this."

That actual response proves my friend has become a financial hostage—one who is caught and bound by financial handcuffs, running on the Hampster Wheel. He confesses that God reigns. Yet he is stressed out, chasing his own independent business pursuits.

This is very serious because his spiritual and personal life is in danger of collapse. I've been there, and I know that no amount of money is worth that risk—for money entices us—it even talks. NOBODY CAN SERVE GOD AND MONEY.

Let's join the Apostle Paul's prayer for us today . . .

"I remember you in my prayers, asking that the God of our Lord Jesus Christ, the Father of glory, give you a spirit of wisdom and revelation in the true knowledge of Him" (Ephesians 1:18, 19).

NO ONE CAN SERVE BOTH

"No one can serve two supreme masters (Lords) for you will have hatred for one of the Lords vs. agape love for the other . . . you cannot serve God and (the spirit of Lord) Mamonas" (Matthew 6:24).

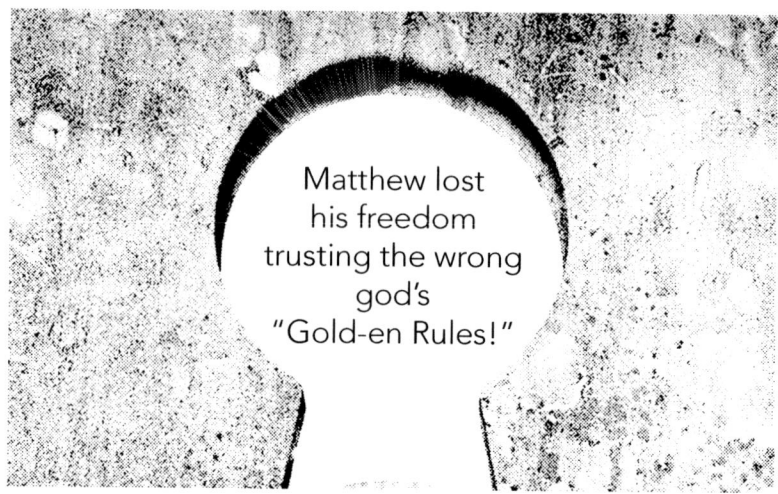

Matthew lost his freedom trusting the wrong god's "Gold-en Rules!"

Matthew the tax collector knew Yeshua's Golden Rule was not practical. The two golden rules that worked for him in the Roman Empire were:

- He who has the gold—makes the rules!
- Do unto others—before they do unto you!

As I mediate on this, I resolve to live in the freedom that comes as I follow the Lord's Golden Rule—treat others the same way I want them to treat me. How encouraging!

GIVE UNTO GOD

I spent many years trying to serve—at the same time—both the spirit of money and the Lordship of Yeshua. What a train wreck that created!

Finally, I understood why my father often quoted from Robert Burns, the national poet of Scotland:
"Mankind are unco weak,
And little to be trusted,
If self the wavering balance tilts,
It's rarely right adjusted!"

It's natural for us to want to tilt "the money scale" in our favor, but first let the Lord's Golden Rule reign: "Do unto others as we want them to do unto us."

I've discovered that the most important thing I can give to God is my life. As Yeshua said, "Give unto God what is God's." Otherwise, we will enter into "darkness."

Let's talk to the Lord and listen for His voice . . .

We pray with the Apostle Paul, "Lord, let us know You and the power of Your resurrection." Your power allows us to profit from our business dealings. We want to benefit from the true riches that only come from You.

DAY 9

THIS PRESENT DARKNESS

My first realization that the devil is the 'god of this world order' was very shocking to me—a game changer! We learn the hard way—by experience—that the devil has many names and great abilities. The names below reflect his plans, objectives and personalities.

The wolf
The destroyer
The crafty serpent
The liar and the father of lies
The ruler of wickedness, who causes iniquity
The prince of the power of the air, working rebellion
The ruler and world-force over this present darkness
The god of this world, whose purpose is to deceive
The thief, who comes to steal, kill and destroy (us)
The ruler of the demons, Beelzebub
The devil's strategies and schemes
The ruler of this world's kingdoms
The prideful one
The dragon

"For our struggle is not against flesh and blood, but against rulers, against powers, against world forces of this [present] darkness, against spiritual forces of wickedness in the heavenly (supernatural) places" (Ephesians 6:12).

SELAH! When I meditate and consider these names, it wakes me up to the reality of who my enemy is. I refuse to give him an opportunity—a foothold—in my life.

BEWARE!

No innocence is strong enough to intimidate Satan. His victims are as numerous as the sands of the sea.

There is: No purity, pure enough to daunt him.
No mercy for the defenseless.
No regard for the truth.
No respect for justice.

In their arrogance, intellectuals and business people often attribute the devil's victims, strategies and iniquities as God's fault. They rail against the Lord in hatred. How deceiving is that? (Psalm 2).

When I started to study God's Word, I discovered the kingdom, strategies and schemes of darkness were designed to work against my businesses, my family and me. Then, I "woke up" to my real need for God's wisdom, blessings and power.

Father God, we recognize we need You today . . .

We want to be "Strong in the Lord and in the strength of Your might." We pray to stand firm against the world's forces of this 'present darkness.' Keep us from compromising in money and our business decisions.

THE POWER OF THE LORD ALMIGHTY

While studying the wonderful and powerful Names of God,
I took a deep breath of relief. What a joy it is to serve . . .

The Lord of lords
The King of kings
The Creator of All Things
The Son of the Living God
The Holy One, Faithful and True
The Author and Finisher of our Faith
The One Who Rules from the Throne
Name Above All Names (Jesus, Yeshua)
Whatever Door He Opens—No One Can Shut!
The Lord Who Gives You the Power to Gain Wealth
He Proclaims Release to the Conquered and Captive
The Great and Chief Shepherd of us, His Sheep
The One Who Gives us Abundant, Eternal Life
He is the Messiah—The Anointed One
The Savior, Who Died for our Sins
The True Light of The World
The Alpha and The Omega
The Rock of All Ages
Wonderful Counselor
The Prince of Peace
The Redeemer
Limitless God

" . . . choose for yourselves whom you will serve . . .
but as for me and my house, we will serve the LORD"
(Joshua 24:15).

*I am encouraged to meditate on His Powerful names.
As I sit here, Father, write them on my heart—now.*

LIMITLESS GOD

One of God's names that stands out to us today is Limitless—He is the Limitless God.

Suppose that light does travel at 186,000 miles per SECOND. At that speed, it takes sunlight an average of 8 minutes and 20 seconds to travel to the Earth. Also consider that The Milky Way is "only" 100,000 light years in diameter. Would you say all of this is limitless from a human standpoint?!

Now we also can call upon the other great names of God with assurance and full confidence that He will answer us. Yeshua's Names indeed have limitless power, leading us to unexpected, limitless opportunities.

Teach us, Lord, to pray at all times . . .

. . . as we talk to You in the Spirit. Keep us alert to stand strong, trusting our prayers will be answered "however You—our Limitless God—see best." We follow Your guidance this day (see Ephesians 6:18).

LIMITLESS & UNEXPECTED

As Matthew counted the money, he heard the crowd coming in the direction of his tax booth. Would Yeshua come by? Matt really wanted to see Him in person. Before he could look up, Yeshua walked in. The crowd leaned forward. Was the unexpected about to happen?

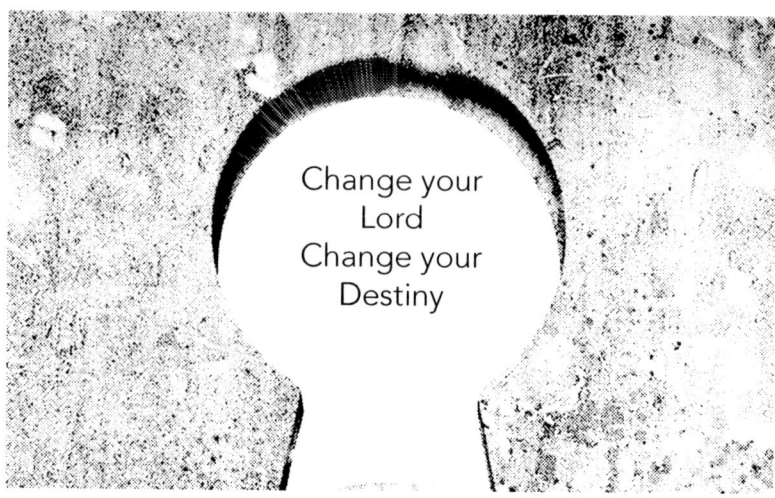

Change your
Lord
Change your
Destiny

Matthew was so shocked; he dropped the tax extortion money he was counting onto the table. Would Yeshua's love and calling be enough to release and redeem him from his love of money and the devil's hold? He never imagined that this day would present his greatest challenge and fabulous . . . but unknown opportunities.

Today, as I stop to meditate, I am reminded that I only want Your challenges and opportunities. Encourage me that they are limitless—just as You are.

OPPORTUNITY

Matthew could not believe his ears. Yeshua looked at Matt as only He could, with all the love of the Son of God, and Matthew heard the words come out of His mouth:

"FOLLOW ME!"

Matthew knew there were two clear opportunities in front of him—he had finally reached the proverbial fork in the road.

> "The opportunity of a lifetime
> Only lasts the lifetime of
> The opportunity!"

I remember the day that my opportunity came to "Follow Him." That day, my life changed from 'limited' to 'limitless.' Eternity also came into view. The weight of the world lifted off my shoulders. The golden handcuffs fell off. Finally free from all the worries, business troubles and my sins, I was forgiven. What a wonderful day!

Lord, this day, we open our hearts . . .

. . . to burn again in response to Your great call and Your great salvation. Lord, give us the power to follow You. Release us, Lord, from our business traps. Fill our hearts with the fire to run with You.

THE GOLDEN HANDCUFFS FALL OFF

I was a financial hostage and in bondage to:
'He who has the gold makes the rules.'
I was handcuffed by my blind ambition.
Thank God, I was released to follow Yeshua.
"If the Son makes you free—free indeed" (John 8:36).

When we feel the grip of the golden handcuffs, let's "Raise up the shield of faith and extinguish all the flaming arrows of the evil one" (Ephesians 6:16).

As I think back upon the power of my blind ambition, I acknowledge its golden handcuffs made me powerless to follow You without reservations. I start this day encouraged—free—full of energy.

LIMITLESS FREEDOM

W hen I read in the Book of Matthew his testimony about leaving behind his money, women, security and worldly status to follow the Lord, I am amazed.

Obviously he realized there was something far greater. Little did he know he was about to discover the Limitless God of the Universe.

BUT—EVEN SO—HOW? How could the Lord, Yeshua:
• Choose someone who had neglected and taken monetary advantage of His own people?
• Give a new fabulous opportunity to someone who had gone the wrong way with the wild crowd?
• Forgive a rich swindler, who served (Lord) Mamonas?
• Choose one for whom 'enough had never been enough?'
• Eat—drink—love & laugh with tax collectors?
• Use one who stole and said—'WELL THAT'S ONLY BUSINESS?'

As we pray, we confess . . .

Father God, You are truly the same yesterday, today and forever. Your unchanging law of love redeems us. Lord, let us experience more of that limitless love and power. Let Your encouragement and confidence guard us.

EAT, DRINK AND BE MERRY

"After Matthew followed Yeshua, he gave a big reception for Him in his house; and there was a great crowd of tax collectors and other immoral people who were reclining at the table with them" (Luke 5:27-29).

A new merry generous heart produces outrageous hospitality

I enjoy watching my friends become free from the deception and lordship of money. Then their JOY comes—free from toil, hurt and pain.

"A joyful heart is a good medicine" (Proverbs 17:22).

SELAH! Pause and consider this: Joy and generosity lead me to stressless wealth.

GENEROUS HEART

Before I was saved, and especially after a lucrative business deal, I always enjoyed eating, drinking and celebrating. However, after I followed the Lord, my merriment had a different center of gravity. Yeshua became the master of ceremonies at my parties.

So after I was saved, what else could I do except throw a party—a big reception in honor of Yeshua. Everyone in the old days knew that Matt did not do things in a reserved way, but neither do I. Just as the Pharisees objected to and complained about Matthew's parties, my skeptics also consider my hospitality to be outrageously generous.

However, truth is truth, and a joyful heart is free and first thinks of others, sharing both abundantly and graciously. Not like the rich young ruler . . .

Thank You, Lord, for freeing our hearts . . .

As we meditate on You, we are encouraged to express our gratitude for Your generous heart and outrageous hospitality toward us. We want to sit at Your banquet table this day and forever!.

THE RICH YOUNG RULER

There comes a time in everyone's life when they ask themselves, "When is enough—ever enough?" One day, we will realize the battle isn't about gaining more wealth. It is about, "Has wealth conquered you?"

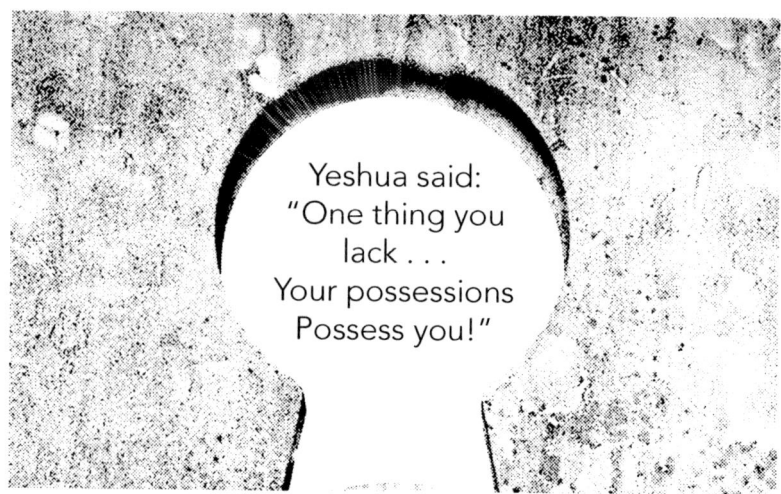

Yeshua said:
"One thing you lack . . .
Your possessions
Possess you!"

"Yeshua said, 'How hard it is for the wealthy to enter the Kingdom of God!' They were shocked, 'Then who can be saved?' Yeshua answered, 'What is impossible with people is possible with God'" (Luke 18:22-27).

Today, I will be still and reflect upon the fact that I am saved from the grip of my possessions. He is my God and nothing is impossible with Him.

ENJOY GENEROUS GIVING

Have you ever been speechless? I have—especially when I first thought about Enjoying Generous Giving.

The rich young ruler was also speechless when Yeshua asked him to give more than what he was willing to part with. It was definitely not the challenge or answer he expected from the 'good teacher.'

The rich young ruler's identity was threatened. He believed that his riches protected his position, image and earthly importance. They were even more valuable to him than eternity.

Don't be confused. Yeshua said, "Those who have left things behind for the sake of the Kingdom will receive many times as much now and in the age to come, eternal life." This statement freed me to enjoy Generous Giving.

As we pray, I am reminded . . .

Lord, touch the mysterious center of our being, our hearts, with the grace, blessing and favor to fully respond to Your call. You've given us so freely and abundantly, so we respond to You by generous giving from a happy heart.

THERE ARE TWO KINGDOMS

For many business people, even Christians, work is in one "kingdom" and the church is in another. These Christians switch between two different personalities—that are not related to each other. But the ultimate 'test question' of life is:

Which Kingdom are you in—which king do you serve?
Tell us—Which is the real you?

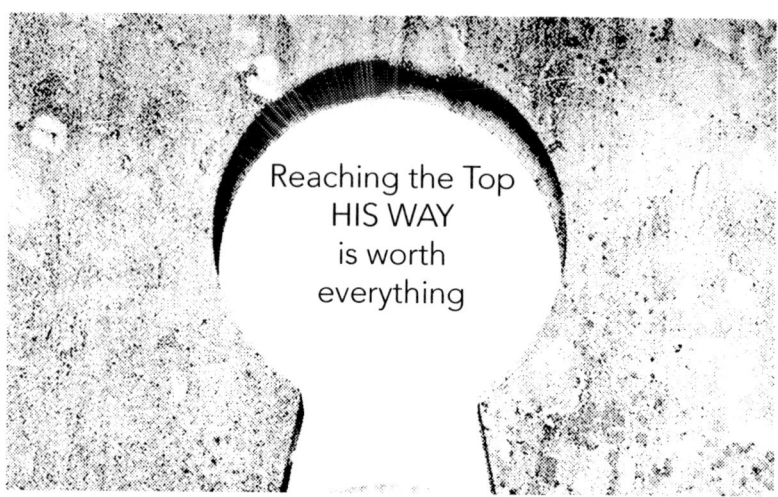

Reaching the Top
HIS WAY
is worth
everything

"Yeshua told His disciples, '. . . most people, while seeing they do not see, and while hearing they do not hear, nor do they understand'" (Matthew 13:13).

As I reflect on this today, I see, hear and understand. Now I break free from the foolishness of trying to live in two separate kingdoms at the same time. I need only one King and Master.

WE ARE IN OPPOSITE ONES

once had a Christian friend whose girlfriend was beautiful and ambitious. She was a real opportunist when it came to making money, using her craftiness and sexy ways to manipulate people. Eventually, even my friend's conscience toward the Lord began to be tainted. Obviously, their relationship was on a collision course.

While having dinner one evening, she said, "I don't care about your religion or your ethics. I'm going to get to the top, no matter the cost! You have convinced me there are two spiritual kingdoms—and we are in opposite ones. I will not let you slow me down." Then the femme fatale stood and shouted, "Good luck and goodbye forever."

I've seen many similar situations, and found there really is no way to avoid the "big conflict"—two different kingdoms are at war. This is a great mystery.

As we come together to pray . . .

Lord Jesus, make us aware of the price You've paid to bring Your Kingdom to Earth. Today, we want a clean conscience with You. We commit ourselves to follow Your Spirit's guidance wholeheartedly, in business and in our personal relationships.

KINGDOM MYSTERIES

When I first studied this Word, it puzzled me. Imagine: ". . . to them who have, more shall be given—in abundance." This means there's a great reward for those who want to be faithful stewards. I want to multiply all that God has entrusted to me.

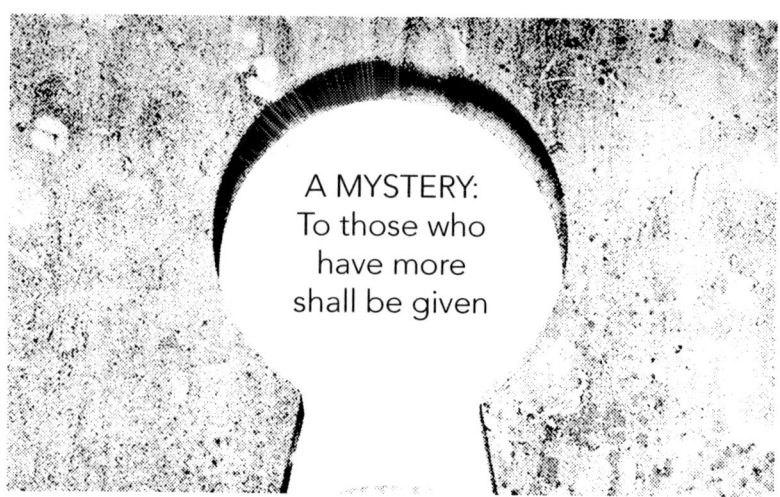

A MYSTERY:
To those who have more shall be given

"To you it has been granted to know the mysteries of the Kingdom, but to them—not granted. Whoever has, more shall be given—an abundance; but whoever does not have, even what he has, shall be taken away" (Matthew 13:11, 12).

What a dramatic truth. SELAH! I now pause and consider this mystery. I want to be one of those who receive—steward—multiply what You've granted me.

TRUST WITH MORE

think I understand that part of the mystery, but for Yeshua to challenge us with His next words is shocking, "For whoever does not have, even what he has, shall be taken away."

No wonder I don't hear this mentioned or discussed. However, this is stated five different times by Yeshua and repeated again at the beginning of His last week on Earth (see Luke 19:24-26).

In today's business world, both of these mysteries are ignored. However, it seems that Yeshua's Words call me to be a faithful multiplier, and one who looks to the future, realizing there are great risks in missing His will, way and results.

Lord, open the eyes of our hearts today . . .

We want to be trustworthy stewards of all that You've given us—not fearful—not lazy—but faithful and diligent. We are encouraged to hear You say, "Well done, good servant—I trust you with even more increase."

LIMITLESS RESULTS

"As the sower sowed, some seeds fell beside the road, and the birds came and ate them up. Others fell on the rocky places—others fell among the thorns—and others fell on the good soil" (Matthew 13:3-8).

Hear His Word
Flourish in
Good Soil
Get 100 X Limitless
Increase

"And the one on whom seed was sown on the good soil, this man hears the word and understands it; who indeed bears fruit and brings forth, some a **hundredfold**, some sixty and some thirty" (Matthew 13:23).

As I meditate, I accept Your powerful challenge to live and flourish in Your good soil of great increase. I also want to be a good listener.

100 X FACTOR INCREASE

've discovered, as God's Word grows in my heart, it brings forth a huge, leveraged increase of Yeshua's blessings—sometimes even a 100 X Factor return.

100 X Factor Increase is available for you!
BELIEVE IT!

Before reading the Parable of the Sower, I thought that God's Kingdom was about leaving things. However, it is also about an exciting, limitless life, full of endless possibilities.

Yeshua focused on the 100 X return—FIRST! But remember that of the four different types of soil, only the seed in the good soil really prevailed. Those who hear, understand and follow the Word of His Kingdom reap abundance. Others will have regrets.

Lord, we really do want to flourish . . .

We admit that we are so limited in the hustle and bustle of our 'ant hill' life when we don't trust our financial affairs to You. Give us Your calm in this hectic day. Keep us in perfect peace. Our minds wait expectedly for Your limitless answers.

HAVE REGRETS?

Many times we look back on situations we regret—wondering, "What was I thinking? How did that happen?" We all make mistakes, lose money and face tragedies. The good news is, God is able to redeem and restore the years we've wasted and even make our past failures work for our good.

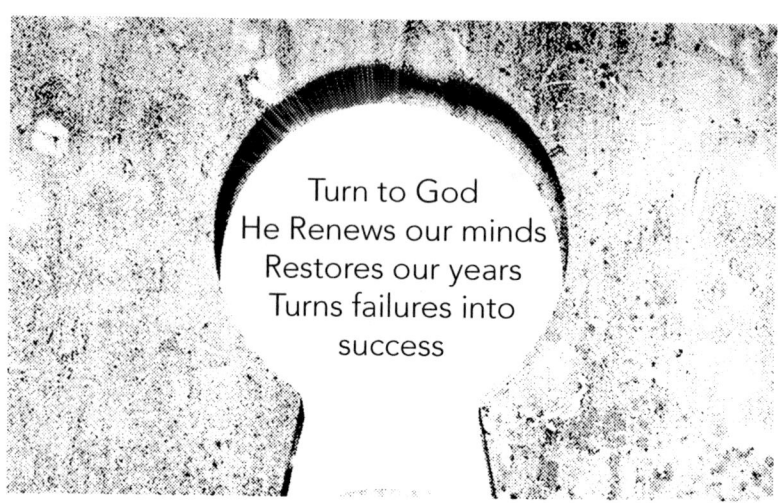

Turn to God
He Renews our minds
Restores our years
Turns failures into
success

"The man who hears the Word, yet has no firm root, stumbles when affliction or persecution arises" (Matthew 13:20, 21).

I am so encouraged that Father God promises to "restore the years the locust has eaten" (Joel 2:25). Today I resolve to receive God's forgiveness and leave my regrets behind. I want my 'roots' to grow deeper and stronger in Him.

SEEKING LOVE & LAUGHTER

When we're ready to recover from our regrets, then any cost is worth paying for 'Love & Laughter'—to become restored and free. Our regrets must be a foreign land to us.

What does it cost to gain 'Love & Laughter?'

- FORGIVE—myself first, then others.
  Forgive 1—set 2 free
- FORGET—leave the bad past behind
- LOVE—yourself first, and then your neighbor
- LAUGH—out loud; it heals the pain
- IDENTIFY—your future with the King
- REMEMBER—He paid for your freedom
- EXPECT—no limits to His answers and generosity
- GIVE—be a blessing

Come back! Walk again with Him!

Lord, we have had many regrets . . .

You know them all. Cleanse our minds. Assure us that our past is forgiven. This moment of prayer comes with a new beginning for us. Your mercies are new every morning. Great is Your faithfulness! (Lamentations 3:22)

WHEN IS ENOUGH

Keep greed far from you . . . it is your enemy. Do not believe the lie that your life is "made up of your possessions." Do not worry. God will supply your every need. His supply has been my long-term experience.

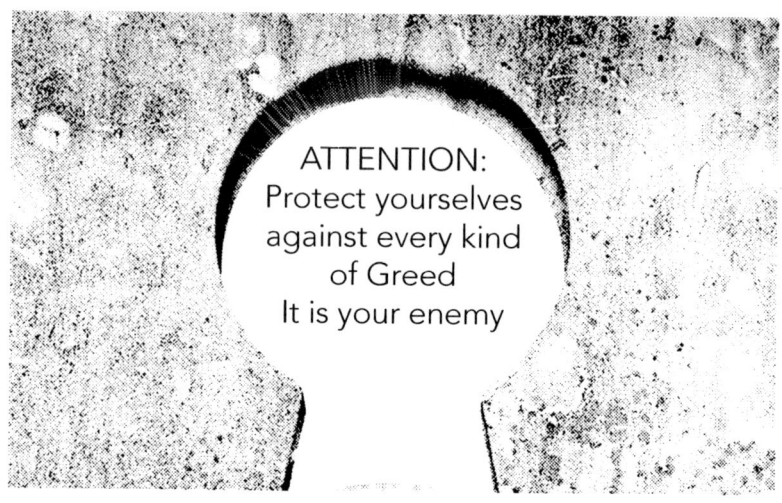

ATTENTION:
Protect yourselves
against every kind
of Greed
It is your enemy

"Yeshua said, 'Beware, and be on your guard against all forms of greed; for even when one has an abundance, his life doesn't consist of his possessions'" (Luke 12:15).

Today I decide to stop worrying about my possessions. I am encouraged I have enough, because You care for me more than I care for myself.

IS THERE EVER ENOUGH?

When I started out in Investment Banking on Wall Street, it was obviously insinuated and definitely practiced that "Greed Is Good!" So many businessmen think that their worth consists of their possessions, and winning is what life is all about!

Yeshua wasn't worried about upsetting anyone when He talked about greed to rich, powerful religious and government leaders. At the height of Yeshua's popularity, He forcefully repeated these unpopular truths!

We feel like we never have enough.
"My barns are not big enough, so I'll tear them down and build bigger barns . . ." (Luke 12:16-21)

Most think that greed is a real motivator to increase commissions and profits. We have a lot of hidden concepts to change. The first one is being appreciative with what we do have.

Lord, help us now with our weaknesses . . .

We are so glad that our provision and peace come from Your Limitless Love, Wisdom and Authority. Cleanse our minds from greed and wrong business concepts. Give us the vision that true prosperity with satisfaction only comes from You.

TEAR DOWN MY BARNS

"A rich man's land was very productive. He reasoned, 'I will tear down my barns and build greater ones to store all my grains and goods. My prosperity will protect me for many years. I'll eat, drink and be merry.'"

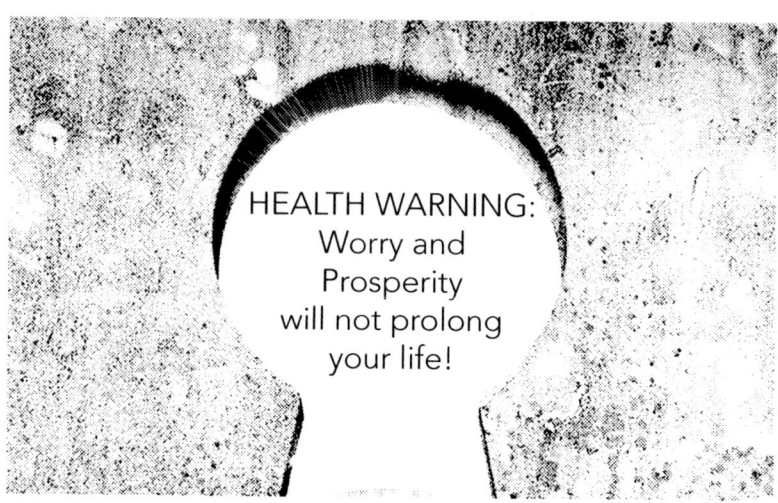

HEALTH WARNING: Worry and Prosperity will not prolong your life!

"God said to him, 'You fool! This very night your soul is required of you; and now who will own what you have prepared?' So it is with the man who stores up treasure for himself, and is not rich toward God" (Luke 12:20, 21).

I realize that if I become truly rich, it's only because of Your favor and generosity. Yeshua, You alone are my very great reward.

BIRDS AND BARNS

"Do not worry about life, what you eat or drink—about your body—what you wear—your wealth. Life and provision—are they not more than food, and the body is more than clothing? Look at the birds of the air. They do not plant or harvest, or have a treasury or barns, and yet your Heavenly Father feeds them.

Do you realize that your worth is much more than the birds?" (Luke 12:22-24).

I so enjoy watching the birds. Actually, I feed them every day; sometimes 15 come at one time. This same picture is what our Heavenly Father paints for us. Birds certainly have no worries and wear the most beautiful 'clothing' imaginable. What a lesson! However, many refuse to see the 'birds' lessons' and become self-consumed and anxious.

Lord, we admit that no amount of worry . . .

. . . or anxiety will add one inch to our height or one single hour to our lifespan. We pray this truth lands in our hearts and minds. We start this day free from false burdens and stressing worries. We trust You in every issue and business dealing.

SELF-CONSUMED GOOD GUYS

"... I say to everyone among you, 'Don't think more highly of yourself than you should. Be honest in your evaluation, measuring yourselves by the faith God has given us and have sound judgment'" (Romans 12:3).

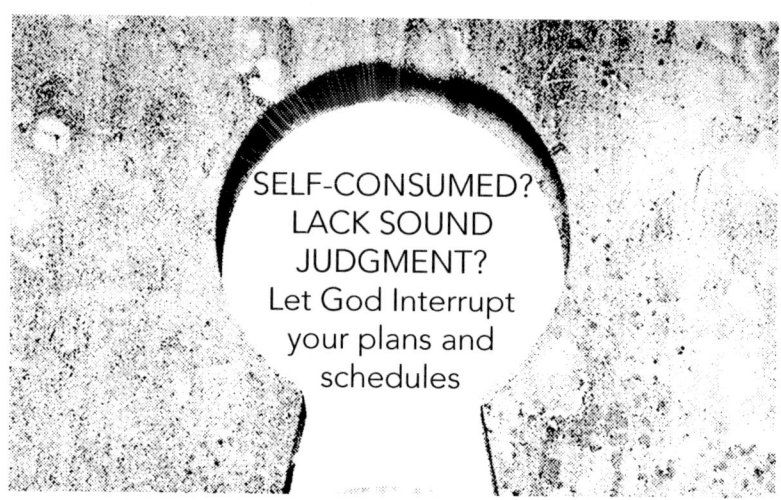

SELF-CONSUMED?
LACK SOUND
JUDGMENT?
Let God Interrupt
your plans and
schedules

Check your motives and critical laughter . . .
"Humble yourselves in the presence of the Lord,
and He will exalt you" (James 4:9, 10).

Today I realize my need to humble myself before the Lord. I want to see myself the way He sees me. May my thoughts be His thoughts—forever and a day.

DIVINE INTERRUPTIONS

I n your prosperity, do you Seek for and Allow Divine Counsel? Can God interrupt your plans?

Usually, by thinking only about themselves, self-consumed business executives create dramas. This doesn't mean that they are cruel to their employees or exclude them from their fabulous parties. Gradually, the irrevocably self-centered and self-seeking become pitiful and boring!

It is normal to have a business plan. However, real conflicts arise when we exclude our projections, expectations and cash-flows from the will, ways and purposes of the Living God.

You know what happened when I started including Yeshua in my decisions? Most of the dramas and insanity attached to them stopped.

Father God, we admit that . . .

The dramas we create are often unnecessary and tiring—save us from them. We need You to interrupt our plans. Thank You for being on our side. As we confess this, we start today encouraged—at peace with You.

SUCCESSFUL INSANITY

A man who creates success by his own intelligence, cleverness and strength is laying up treasures that won't last. God says to the man who blindly trusts in **Me, Myself & I,** "You fool! This night your soul is required of you—now who will own what you prepared?"

If we forget
God's blessings
they forget us

Do you know any examples of 'successful insanity?' I was one. This term applied to me at the beginning of my business career. I believed that many of the blessings I had came from my own brilliance and shrewd negotiations. **How foolish is trusting that?!**

As I meditate upon this today, I am encouraged to let go of trusting my own understanding. Instead, help me trust Your ways first—above mine.

CHASING THE "GOD OF GOLD"

"Then Moses returned to the Lord and said, 'This people has committed a great sin. They have made a god of gold to worship'" (Exodus 32:31).

At one time, I foolishly pursued serving gold. At first this 'god' seemed to serve me; then I became its slave.

Eventually, I remembered what the Lord had taught about the deceitfulness of riches, which in their own creative ways cause most of the worries of life.

I now attribute the god of gold as the creator of the proverbial 'hamster wheel.' Because once its pursuit gets us on the 'wheel of fortune,' our blind ambition keeps us from getting back to the opportunities that God creates, blesses and uses.

Running on the wheel of fortune seems like such a . . .

. . . glamorous and exciting way to make a living. But Lord, call us into Your Kingdom of righteous thinking. We pray, Father God, keep us off the glittering 'wheels' offered to us by the 'gods of gold'.

BLIND AMBITION

There is NO peaceful coexistence between
God's Purpose, Plan and Provision for you
VS
the devil's destructive strategies and schemes—
used to deceive and destroy many.

"Why did I make such a stupid decision?" I was dumb
enough to answer, "It just seemed like the right thing to
do at the time." Our blind ambitions are so flawed it is
easy for the devil to deceive us with our own emotional
impulses.

*Today, I turn my thoughts toward You. I am
encouraged You alone save me from my own stupid
decisions and the devil's deception. I mediate on Your
Word to renew my mind.*

IF YOU CAN'T REFUSE

att, the tax collector turned disciple, responded, "Wow! What happened next?" Yeshua continued, "The devil took me to a high mountain and showed me all the kingdoms of the world, saying, 'All this glory (and kingdoms) I will give to You—for it has been handed over to me—if You fall down and worship me. ALL YOURS!'" (Matthew 4:1-11).

The 'enemy,' through his subtlety, often convinces us that when we bow down to him, in the end, the prosperity will be worth it. That's what his desire is—to bring an end to the power of God in our lives. That happens if we can't refuse the devil's offers.

The devil comes to kill, steal and destroy by offering us money, position and glory. This deceives, distracts and delays us from learning God's lessons.

Today, we join in the Apostle Paul's prayer:

May the eyes of my heart be opened and enlightened, that I will know the hope of His calling me (Ephesians 1:16, 18).

LIFE IS A SCHOOL

Yeshua's lesson at the Sermon on the Mount was about 'the broad gate—the world's way that leads to destruction.' I thought, "Ouch!" However, my questions were clarified after reading, "For the gate is narrow—the way of His will for me—that leads to life, and few find it" (Matthew 7:13, 14).

TAKE YOUR PICK:
You can't serve
BOTH
It's either the
Lord God
or (Lord) Mamonas

I imagine my 'old friend Matt, the tax collector,' at first wished he'd never heard that! I picture him leaving his tax office, remembering that challenging admonishment.

As I prayed the prayer on the next page, I learned the lessons that changed my selfish business life.

Today, join me in encouragement and purpose that comes from this prayer:

NEW PRAYER—NEW PURPOSE

"Our Father, Holy and Glorious is Your Name . . . Your Kingdom come . . . So please, Father King . . .

Your Will be accomplished in our lives. Your desires are better than ours.

Your will, as in Heaven, be done on Earth.

You are our bread, our supply, our provision—today and tomorrow.

Please forgive us—for we forgive others. (After forgiveness comes Your blessing.)

Over temptations, give us Your power, Your purpose. Keep us from falling prey to glittering offers.

Deliver us from the business principalities, lies and deceptions of the evil one.

Help us overcome with Your love, power, dominion and glory.

Keep us close—never let us go." (see Matthew 5, 6, 7)

LOVE POWER™

" . . . He might test you, to do good for you—in the end. Otherwise, you may say in your heart, 'My power and the strength of my hand made me all this wealth.' But it is the Lord Who gives you power to make wealth by Covenant . . .'" (Deuteronomy 8:12-20).

God's Love Power
frees us
from Money's
Power

The love of money and its power makes us deaf to God's voice. When we follow money's voice, we go after other gods, seek and serve them. God testifies against us that if we do so, we will surely perish. Money votes for itself— exposing us.

Today, I am encouraged Your 'Love Power' also includes the power to make wealth. Save me from money's talk.

GUARD YOUR HEART

Moses was clear: "When you build good houses and your flocks multiply, your silver and gold multiply, and all that you have multiplies, then your heart will become proud, and you will forget the Lord your God Who brought you out of the house of slavery."

I've discovered that trusting in my own identity, security and possessions does just that—it makes me proud—puts me at risk of going back to the 'house of slavery.' This admonishment of Moses is a good reminder.

It is of ultimate importance to guard our hearts with wisdom. "Guard your heart and love wisdom, and it will watch over you"—wise words from King Solomon. Otherwise, money consumes our time and life leaves us empty. Instead, we set our affection on things above and accept no limits.

Our fickle hearts want . . .

. . . the things of this world. We pray today, teach us to watch over our hearts with all diligence, for from them flow the issues of life, health and prosperity.

LIMITLESS DIVINE PLANS

'"For I know the plans that I have for you,' declares the Lord, 'plans for prosperity and not for calamity, to give you a future and a hope'" (Jeremiah 29:11).

For I
alone know
—your plans—
I MADE THEM!

"I want you to know My plans, that it is I, the Lord, the God of Israel, Who calls you by your name. I will give you the treasures of darkness—and hidden wealth of secret places" (Isaiah 45:3).

Today, I think about Your plans and the treasures You have for my life—limitless, if I dare to ask. I am very encouraged to remember how much You care for me.

FULFILL YOUR DESTINY

Yeshua halted and looked up into the sycamore tree at a very shocked Zaccheus. "Hurry down, little man! I must visit your home today" (Luke 19:1-10).

Have you ever been 'the skeptic,' hiding in the tree, watching for Yeshua but not wanting Him to see you? I have! I've also wondered, like Zaccheus, if the Lord could do something good for me. In Jericho, others also wondered why Yeshua would want to visit the home of a corrupt, immoral chief tax collector, the shrewdest money man in the Jordan Valley.

However, Yeshua always has a Divine Plan and someone's destiny in mind. He sees a persons' heart and their limitless possibilities—not the rumors and judgments of others.

Dear reader, may God help you understand His mysterious power, plan and destiny for you, your business and your family.

Others cannot see what we could be . . .

So Lord, thank You that You do. What limitless plans You have for us! We pray to receive this Word. Give us the strength to fulfill our calling, prosperity and destiny!

THAT MYSTERIOUS POWER

"And he called ten of his slaves, and gave them ten minas and said, 'Do business with this until I come back.' When he returned, he called them to know what business they had done." These words amaze me. Yeshua challenges His servants to do business.

Do business
with 'My money'
Big Prosperity
Big Rewards

"The first appeared (to answer His challenge), 'Lord, Your one Mina has made ten more.' He said, 'Well done (NOT WELL TAUGHT, WELL SPOKEN or WELL BELIEVED) . . . WELL DONE good slave, being faithful with 'My money' brings authority—rewards—ruling over ten cities'" (Luke 19:12-26).

I have never considered that Your one 'Mina' could make a 1,000% increase.

'YOUR' MINA

On the first day of His final week, Yeshua introduced this fantastic and important story. His servants had to give an account of the business they had done with 'His Money.' The first one received the largest reward.

Yeshua's offer of different rewards—based on different results—was a brand new concept. Yeshua has challenged me with the same opportunity to use His money for Kingdom building and His business purposes.

The mysterious power of using His money for business is a secret we do not often hear discussed. What a shocking new standard! The first servant said to the Lord, "Your money—not my brilliance—not my business acumen alone— has made 10 X more.

YOUR MONEY . . . NOT MY MONEY."
That servant was happily rewarded.

Expand our minds . . .

C. S. Lewis challenged us, "Aslan is not a tame lion . . . he is wild—that lion is not safe, but he is good." Lord, we pray to know You in new and different ways. We want Your rewards and to be rulers over many 'cities.'

LOOK AT THE BIRDS

Consider this:
"Aren't two little birds sold for a penny? Don't you realize you are more valuable than many little birds, so don't fear; you must be confident in how much more He watches over you" (Matthew 10:29-31).

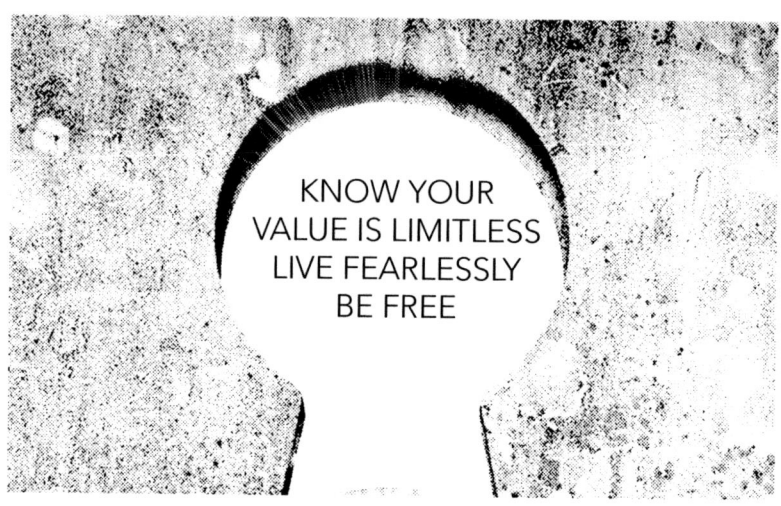

KNOW YOUR
VALUE IS LIMITLESS
LIVE FEARLESSLY
BE FREE

"Those who wait on the Lord will renew their strength (and be freed to) soar with wings like the eagles" (Isaiah 40:31).

I close my eyes right now and picture Your fresh wind blowing over my wings, and off I soar. How encouraging it is to be one of Your eagles in Your limitless skies.

TRUST YOUR 'FEATHERS'

Did you know that the feathers of the eagle are not only beautiful, but each one of them is hand painted? We are created and sculptured even more amazingly. Yet, we need to learn from the birds how they use their delicate, beautiful feathers to soar against the powerful winds.

When I often faced the volatile storms of life, it used to scare me. But then I learned to use the challenging power of those storms to lift my altitude above earthly problems. This changed everything. Now I understand all that was against me, God has used to make me confident, effective and prosperous.

Dear Reader, come soar with me—the great winds are actually for us. With them we fly 1,000 miles nonstop. Whether you are a little sparrow or a big eagle, it takes God's wind and your 'feathers' to confidently fly high.

Lord, we are so encouraged . . .

To wait here with You today. We will not fear the wind and the dark sky any longer. We choose to fly with You this very day—and use the 'feathers' You have given us to soar.

DO NOT BEG

"Do not be anxious or concerned, but in everything by prayer, asking with thanksgiving, let God know your desires and requests. Then the matchless, unfathomable peace of God will guard and protect your hearts and minds in Yeshua" (Philippians 4:6, 7).

In CONFIDENCE
we ask—
In TRUST we receive
Your blessings

"We have confidence to freely speak before Him. We can openly ask anything. If it's according to His will, He hears us. We know if He hears us in whatever we ask, we receive the requests we have asked from Him"
(1 John 5:14, 15).

Lord, as I meditate on these Words, I realize I so often lack the confidence or take the time to freely speak to You about every little and big thing.

LIMITLESS RIGHTS

D o not beg. Instead, come like a business executive would and present to the Boss the checks that need to be signed, the payroll due, the bank records. Be sure that the Boss knows the matters you put before Him need His immediate response and supply. This is the way we should approach our Father God.

He has limitless supply, but in order to claim our rights, it is necessary to use faith with our asking. Our personal relationship with Him is vital for our assurance and confidence that our provision comes from the house of prayer.

I believe the Words in Matthew 7:7-11, which I paraphrase: "Ask, and it will be given to you; when you seek, you will find; keep knocking, then the answer will make sense to you."

Lord, we come boldly before You . . .

We know You long to answer our requests because You said, "Ask and it will be given to you." We ask that our requests are what You would want us to pray. We choose Your decisions in all of our business endeavors.

THE BUYERS AND SELLERS

On the last week of His life, Yeshua entered the Temple. He drove out all those who were buying and selling, overturning the 'money changers' tables and the seats of those who were selling doves" (Matthew 21:8-14).

First GREED
EXCESS PROFITS
Then STEALING—
That's the Temple's
Robbers' Den

"And He said to them, 'It is written, 'MY HOUSE SHALL BE CALLED A HOUSE OF PRAYER;' but you are making it a ROBBERS' DEN." Imagine the greedy, the excessive, the stealers had become 'the staff and approved merchants' of the Temple's trading tables.

As I meditate today, it is sorrowful to imagine the greedy, the envious, the excessive, the robbers that had taken over Your house. I am humbled and so sorry that this happens to You. Save me from being that type of person.

THE ROBBERS' DEN

The last day of Yeshua's public ministry on Earth is, in my opinion, obviously one of the most important. This was His last opportunity to make certain points.

Earlier in the week, He had urged His disciples to buy and sell and do business with HIS Money. So why was He so upset about buying and selling in the Temple? Why did He drive out all of those 'certified merchants' and overturn the tables of the 'money changers?' Isn't trading money just a normal function of the world's business system and its wealth codes?

But the Temple's wealth codes had become obsessive—twisted by greed—excess profits—shamelessly stealing in public. No wonder Yeshua became violent—He was first about His Father's business and House.

Now it becomes clear . . .

Father God, we want to be a righteous and honorable people with good reputations—being about Your business according to Your standards. We pray to become Your stewards in all that You have called us to be. Save us from the corruption of hypocrisy.

ENDLESS POSSIBILITIES

We've come to the last pages of our daily Limitless Living encouragements and meditations. So, let's sum up again: where does Limitless Living begin? From God's breath of Life. It was given to us when God breathed into man His very breath—eternity—limitlessness.

Continuous fellowship with God is Limitless Living

"He has made everything beautiful in its place and time. He has rooted eternity into our hearts, yet man will wear himself out before he discovers the work—design of God—from the beginning to the end" This is one definition of Limitless. (Ecclesiastes 3:11)

As I meditate on this today, I am encouraged that my possibilities are endless. I want to live in continuous worship and fellowship with You.

ATTITUDE = ALTITUDE

P roverbs 23:7 states, "For as you think in your heart so are you." Your predetermined attitude will show on your face, expressing what you expect to get from and give to life—nothing more—nothing less. Are you expecting enough?

God often takes the good expectations we have and increases them. That's why it is so important to start out with an abundant and generous mindset about successful, profitable, limitless living. You'll discover it is true: "He is able and wants to do far more exceedingly, abundantly beyond ALL that we ask or think—dream or imagine—according to His power at work within us" (Ephesians 3:20).

Renew our hearts and change our thinking today . . .

Lord, we want to be all You want us to be. We know that our 'attitude determines our altitude.' Our poor attitude limits Your power in us. Forgive us for our puny requests. Encourage us to expect Your limitless answers now.

ACKNOWLEDGMENTS

In January 2010, after speaking to a group of marketplace leaders in Mumbai, India, a fashion designer came up to me and intensely said, "I just realized I am a financial hostage. Please stay longer or come back soon!" Neither one was an option, but I did want him to know the mysteries of the Kingdom—"For whoever has shall more be given."

I realized if I wrote books with spiritual wisdom and practical advice, learned from being in over 100 business deals, I could not only reach him, but many others.

Right then in Mumbai—my "clarity and calling" came—and the writing of the first book, Breaking The Wealth Code, was conceived. Now, years later, thankfully, many books are coming to life.

Jonathan Shibley, the President of Global Advance was with me when this happened in India. Thank you for your encouragement since then. You are a dear friend.

Many other people spent hours discussing concepts and strategies. They assisted in developing styles, artwork, graphics and promotional videos for Europe and America.

My sincerest appreciation to the European group: Antonio Morra, Dr. Silke Pietsch, Wilfried Franz, Joe Hartung, Giorgio Lombardo and Pastor Nicola Spuria,

Pastor Marco and Angela Palma, Dr. Richard and Eleonore Kogelnig.

Thanks to my American colleagues: Carlos Bido, filmmaker; Andrew Summey, my Israel connection; and both Golan Lindsay and Ed Bianchi of Christ For The Nations, Dallas, Texas.

Finishing the editing, graphics and final shaping of this project was made possible by Maria Erokhina of Volgograd, Russia, Carlos Bido and Polly Harder of Dallas. Polly, I want to thank you for your tremendous ability to get things done in the most time-productive way. Again, we have reached higher and accomplished more than I thought possible. I recommend you with the highest possible rating!

ABOUT THE AUTHOR

Robert M. Saunders, Jr. became the 4th generation of investment bankers. He grew up in a close and loving family along the mighty Mississippi River in Memphis, Tennessee.

July 1952—His spirit of adventure came alive at six years old, when Rob's grandmother, who lived next to the world's largest free zoo, began sending him, with a sack lunch every Saturday, solo, on a zoo 'safari.'

September 1952—He has clear memories of singing this song in Sunday School: "Red and Yellow, Black and White, they are precious in His sight, Jesus loves the little children of the world," and he believed that. Maybe that's why he has traveled to and enjoyed people in over 90 countries.

June 8, 1961—Young Life Camp Frontier Ranch, Buena Vista, Colorado. Rob has the original letter he wrote his parents telling them that he now loved Jesus, "You don't know how thankful I am for Jesus." That will be on his tombstone.

August 1968—he graduated from the University of Colorado, School of Business. During his senior year, he was investing and trading stocks for some of his professors.

After serving as a Captain, and flying with the Military Airlift Command of the United States Air Force, including TDY in Vietnam, he joined his family's investment banking business. He initially specialized in oil and gas deals.

July 23, 1978—He was in a Richmond Christian Fellowship meeting when the Word of God came upon him through the inspiration of the chapter of Isaiah 57, especially verse 18, "I have seen his ways, but I will heal him. I will lead him and restore comfort to him . . . and his mourners."

Rob continued traveling, mentoring and encouraging leaders and college students with the Good News, and founded a campus church at Virginia Commonwealth University.

June 1990—Rob took his family to live and minister in the Soviet Union. They found themselves in the middle of the coup when the hard-line communists arrested Gorbachev in 1991.

December 31, 1999—Rob was living and ministering in Innsbruck, Austria.

January 2001—Freda Lindsay, co-founder of Christ For The Nations would often pray Jeremiah 33:3 over Rob, then they would discuss, "Call upon me and I will answer you and tell you great and mighty things, which you do not know."

February 10, 2006—At a Morning Star Ministries' Prophecy Conference in Fort Mill, South Carolina, he was sitting next to Rick Joyner and Jack Deere. Suddenly Jack asked Rob to be prophesied over—amazing prophecies followed. One that was written really stuck with him:

"Is that a sword? I saw a sword in the shadows, it was lying down. Then a door was opened in the distance and the light shown down from the door onto the sword. After the light hit the sword, it rose up into the air—shining, floating, pointing down. Then I heard the words, 'The Word is being activated—a new authority.'"

February 2008 to present—Robert ministers around the world and at Marketplace Leadership conferences, often with Jon Shibley or Wilfried Franz, while building successful international media publishing companies.

February 2015—Rob's apartment in Rome, Italy, was directly across from the Colosseum. From this inspiring view he studied the history of the Roman Empire and how their far-reaching Pax Romana became the basis of business and trade. His main questions were, "Why did all roads lead to Rome?" And "Why was there continuous conflict between Rome and Jerusalem?" The answers Rob discovered are now woven into his novels and books.

April 4, 2015—While at a Easter GSC Conference (generazionesenzaconfini.com) in the Naples area, ministering along with Loren Cunningham from YWAM, a girl named Valentina gave him this prophecy:

"Robert, this is the word for you: 'In a moment of prayer God showed me your feet. He says, 'STOP!' and take off your shoes before you go because in front of you there's a holy place, a wide road—golden, shiny and sparkling. God also showed me your heart is in His hands.'"

Loren looked at Rob and said, "That is a true prophecy, and there is only one thing that can screw it up—That's YOU!"

May 20, 2016—At Robert Saunders Wood's graduation, the Word of the Lord came to Rob: "For thus says the Lord, 'When 70 years are completed for you in Babylon, I will visit you and keep and fulfill my good word and promises to you . . .'" Jeremiah 29:10.

This was given two months before Rob's 70th birthday. If you would like Rob to speak at your conference or coach in your nation, go to:

robsaunders.com
wealthcodescoach.com
destinymedia.us

We also recommend:

ROB SAUNDERS

BREAKING THE WEALTH CODE

Open your eyes
to riches never
dreamed of...

ROB SAUNDERS

THE **WEALTH CODE** REVEALED

Open your eyes to riches never dreamed of...

Daily Meditations

Power of Purpose, Opportunity Rewards, Decisions Drama, Destiny

COMING SOON:

robsaunders.com
wealthcodescoach.com
destinymedia.us

COMING SOON:

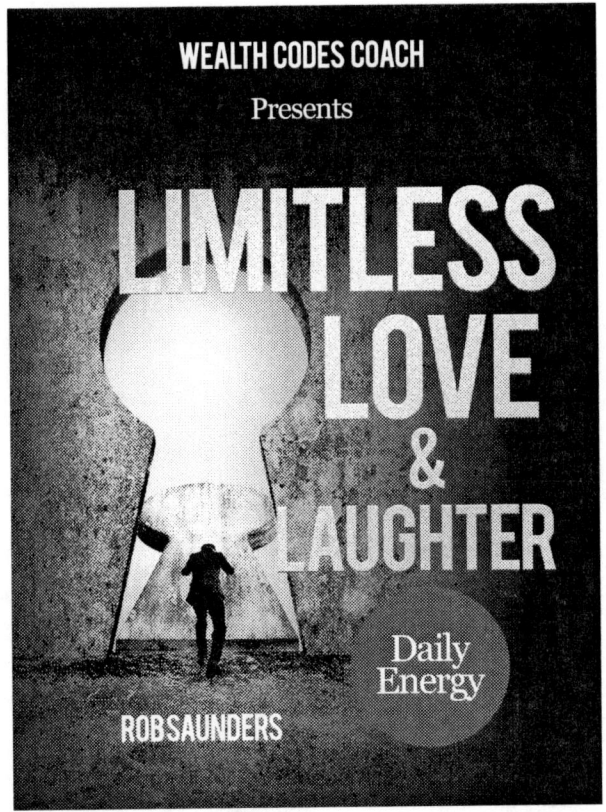

robsaunders.com
wealthcodescoach.com
destinymedia.us